A Visitor's Guide

TO THE PLANTS OF MUIR WOODS NATIONAL MONUMENT

STEVE CHADDE
GLADYS L. SMITH

A Visitor's Guide to the Plants of Muir Woods National Monument

Steve Chadde
Gladys L. Smith

Printed in the United States of America.

ISBN: 978-1951682729

A Pathfinder Field Guide
Published by Orchard Innovations
Mountain View, Arkansas
Author email: *steve@orchardinnovations.com*

version 1.0 01/2023

Contents

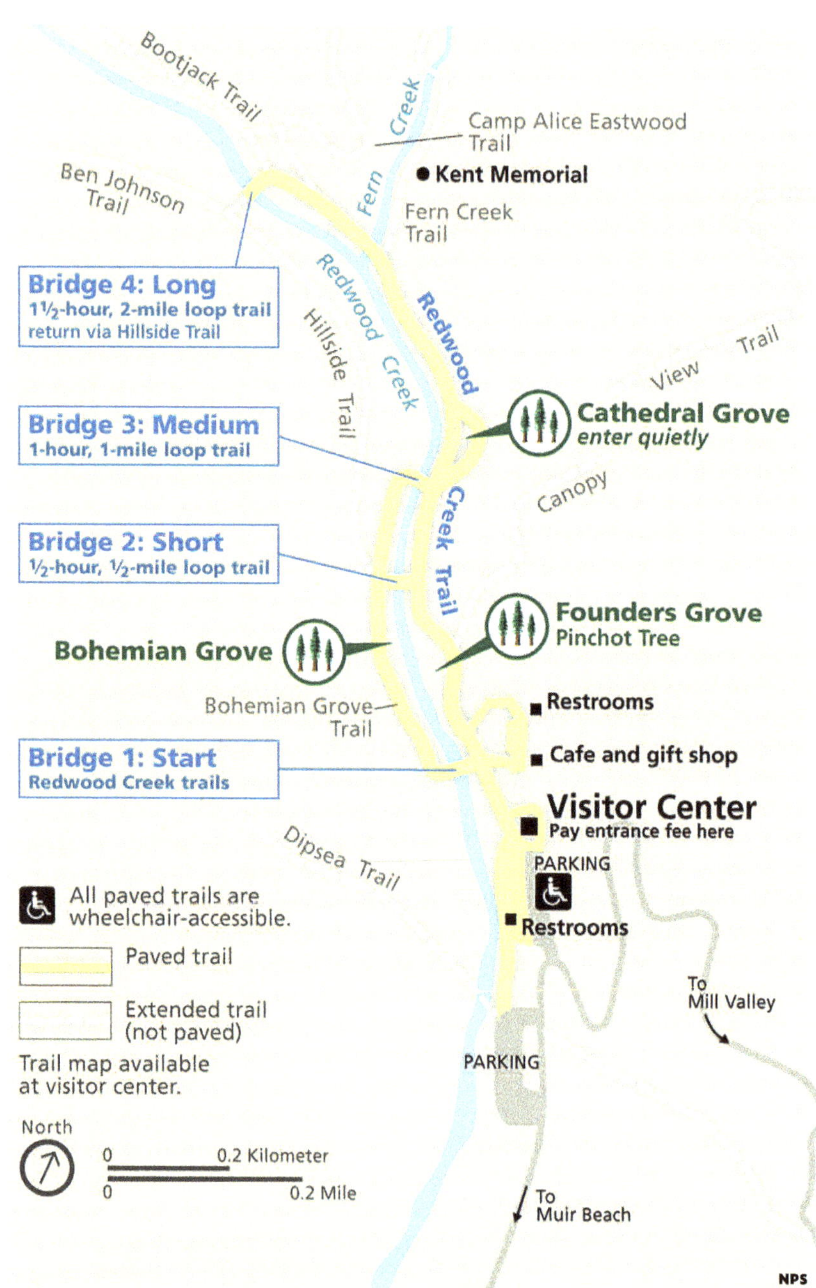

ABOVE Muir Woods National Monument (main area).

Introduction

Muir Woods National Monument was established in 1908 as an outstanding botanical reserve of native plants. Along its quiet shaded paths, not only the redwood trees, its most famous attraction, but also the ferns, shrubs and wildflowers may be observed. Located on the lower flanks of Mount Tamalpais, the Monument is in a canyon cut by the docile-appearing stream known as Redwood Creek. After heavy winter rains, however, this little stream and its tributaries at times go on rampages that even today continue to modify the face of Muir Woods. The soft soils of the steep canyon walls have washed down over countless years to form a rich, deep, alluvial bottomland which supports a luxurious undergrowth of herbaceous plants shaded by the giants for which the monument is known far and wide.

The ever-falling leaves and branches of the forest trees form a thick, cushiony mat that protects and preserves soil moisture even in the rainless months of summer. The assemblage of plants found here is undoubtedly further influenced by the characteristic morning fogs that occur during this otherwise dry summer season, and which at times leave the trees and underplants dripping as though with rain. These summer fogs, together with fairly heavy winter rainfall, provide a suitably moist environment for shade-loving plants which intermingle to form an undergrowth below the redwoods.

The colorful flower fields for which California is famous cannot be attributed to Muir Woods. Here, in the cathedral-like corridors of light and shadow, often only a few plants of a given species may be present within the entire area of the Monument, and only a few of the plants described here could be described as truly abundant. Scattered though they may be, the plants that make up the flora of Muir Woods succeed one another in a bloom period that stretches from January to October, a flowering time that is surpassed in few other places.

The monument lies for the most part within a forested area. Many trails, however, extend into the chaparral vegetation on the higher slopes before reaching boundary lines (see maps, pages 4 and 8). The plants on these upper, relatively exposed slopes, are often colorful and interesting, and a number of them have been included in this book. Since the ferns are conspicuous among the undergrowth plants, these, too, have been included in a section following the flowering plants (page 78).

How to use this book

This book presents the most conspicuous and representative plants of Muir Woods in such a manner that they can be recognized without the use of a botanical key. In all, 77 plants have been selected, which include 64 flowering plants, and 13 ferns, (including the giant horsetail).

As of the time of publication (January 2023), 287 vascular plant species are reported by the National Park Service to occur or are likely to occur within the boundaries of the Monument (see list, page 93). Mosses and lichens, an important part of the Muir Woods flora, are not treated here.

Following the section on common **trees and shrubs**, the sections are next arranged by the predominant color of the flower: 2) **white**, which includes white to cream; 2) **yellow**, which includes pale yellow to orange; 3) **red**, which includes pink through rose-purple; 4) **blue**, which includes blues, lavenders, and purples, and 5) **browns**.

Because there is so much color variation in flowers, such a system of grouping does not always result in a clean-cut decision. Flowers that are white when they first open may become tinged with pink or lavender with age. Or, a flower such as the iris, placed here in the blue section, may also occur as creamy-white. The list is not long, however, and each plant is illustrated by a color photograph. By using the illustrations as well as the color guide, the search for an unknown flower should therefore not be difficult.

The listing of months at the end of each description indicates the **flowering period** for that plant.

Following the wildflower sections are descriptions of all species of **ferns** known to occur in the Monument (beginning on page 78).

Within each section, the plants have been arranged alphabetically by the scientific name of their family. Thus, plants in the same family and with similarly colored flowers will be grouped together. A list of all known vascular plant species, prepared by the National Park Service, begins on page 93. In that list, plants described and illustrated in this book are indicated in bold type and cross-referenced to the book's page number.

An **index** of scientific and common names begins on page 103.

Scientific terms have been used as little as possible and these are listed below.

Bract: a leaflike structure at the base of a flower stem or flower cluster.

Epiphyte: a plant that grows on another plant but is not nourished by it.

Frond: the leaf of a fern.

Fruits: botanically, all seed vessels are referred to as fruits, which actually are matured ovaries and all they contain.

Panicle: an open and branched cluster of flowers.

Perennial: a plant that has a woody root system and that lives and blossoms year after year as compared to an annual which grows from seed, blossoms, matures, and dies in a single season.

Petiole: a leaf stem.

Petals: inner flower envelope, usually colored and showy, which altogether are called the *corolla*.

Sepals: outer flower envelope, usually green, which altogether are called the *calyx*. The calyx usually enfolds the corolla, but in the absence of petals, the sepals themselves often become the showy structure which is called the flower.

Sori: (singular, *sorus*) the fruit-dots of a fern.

Spore: the fruiting body of a fern that corresponds to the seed of a flowering plant.

As a final note, Steve Chadde would like to acknowledge the original author of this book, Gladys L. Smith (1909-1997), who first published a version of this book in 1963 as: *Flowers and Ferns of Muir Woods*. Mrs. Smith was an alumna of the University of the Pacific and had a degree in botany from San Francisco State College. For some years she was with the botany research staff of the California Academy of Sciences. She worked as a field naturalist instructor for the public schools and as a ranger-naturalist for the National Park Service. Mrs. Smith also wrote several additional books, including *Flowers of Lassen* (1962), *A Flora of the Tahoe Basin and Neighboring Areas* (1973), and *A Flora of the Vascular Plants of Mendocino County, California* (1992).

This new work updates the scientific names for all species to those most commonly accepted today, adds a number of plants not in the original edition, and includes all new color photographs. Photographs were used under Creative Commons commercial use licenses, and the author extends his gratitude to those documenting the natural world and making their work available for publication.

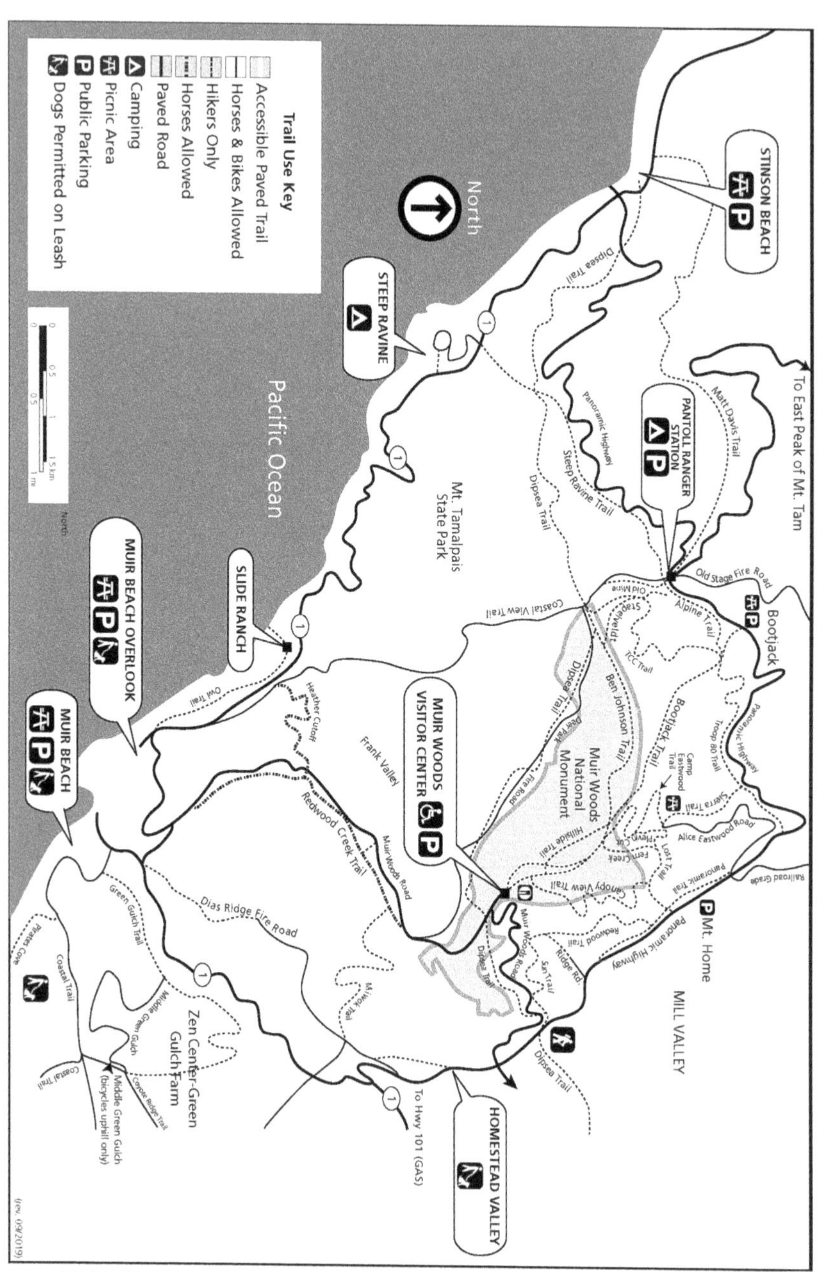

ABOVE Muir Woods National Monument and surrounding area.

Trees and Shrubs

MATHEW DILLON

CRICKET RASPET

ABOVE Autumn leaves, FACING PAGE Fruit

Western Poison-oak

ANACARDIACEAE

Toxicodendron diversilobum

Sumac Family

SYNONYM *Rhus diversiloba*

This common and attractive plant grows either as a shrub or vine, often attaching itself to trees by aerial roots where it climbs to heights of 40 feet and more. In the spring, delicate sprays of cream-colored flowers perfume the air. In autumn, poison-oak is our only plant whose leaves turn brilliant red. Its oak-shaped leaves in 3's give the plant its common name. Direct contact with the oily surfaces of stems or leaves can cause a skin irritation which often appears as watery blisters; it pays to learn to recognize poison-oak in all its variable forms! However, honey made from the flower nectar contains no poison.

FLOWERING April–June

MATT BERGER

Western Poison-Oak

JOHN HASKINS

Oregon-grape BERBERIDACEAE

Mahonia nervosa Barberry Family

This spreading and attractive plant is distinguished by its glossy, hollylike leaflets edged with spiny teeth. An evergreen shrub, it adds to the all-year pattern of low woody plants so characteristic of Muir Woods. Clusters of greenish-yellow flowers stand in stiff, erect racemes at the summits of

CALEB CATTO

UPPER Flowers, LOWER Fruit

main stems. These give way in late summer to blue frosted berries, edible but very sour. From the bright yellow wood, which extends to root parts, Indians made a brilliant yellow dye; the bitter bark of the roots was used medicinally in making a tonic said to relieve numerous ailments.

FLOWERING April–June

BEN KEEN

ABOVE Leaves
RIGHT Female fruit (cones)

JOHN HASKINS

Red Alder — BETULACEAE

Alnus rubra — Birch Family

Red alder survives in the Monument by growing along streams, where it can arch over the water to capture available sunlight. This small tree has smooth, light gray to whitish bark, and wavy-margined leaves. Flowers are either male or female, and borne in separate clusters on the same plant. Male flowers are grouped into an elongate catkin; female flowers are grouped into a shorter, rounded, cone-like structure. The common name and *rubra* refer to the reddish-brown heartwood and inner bark, long used traditionally as a dye. The wood was also prized for making plates and utensils, and the wood was favored for smoking fish.

FLOWERING February–April

BARBARA B

California Honeysuckle

CAPRIFOLIACEAE

Lonicera hispidula

Honeysuckle Family

In the spring when flowery vines entwine trees and shrubs, or in the fall when shiny scarlet berries take their place, the native honeysuckle is as charming and attractive as the better known exotic garden plant. Ours is a woody vine with long slender stems that often climb to 30 feet on any plant that will provide support. Opposite leaves are short-stemmed and those at tips of branches are usually united around the stem. The sprays of purplish-pink flowers are arranged in whorls. It is a frequent plant along boundaries of the Monument.

FLOWERING May–July

PEGANUM

Western Burningbush

CELASTRACEAE

Euonymus occidentalis

Bittersweet Family

Although a member of a large and widespread genus, this interesting shrub is the only representative in western America and occurs but sparingly in California. The slender, straggly branches have opposite leaves abruptly pointed at their tips. Dark brownish-purple flowers about ¼ inch across appear in June. The fruits are quite conspicuous. Seeds are encased in a bright red, deeply lobed *aril* (a fleshy pulp-like structure). Because of these vermillion-colored fruits the plant is often called pawn-broker bush. It is a trailside plant between Cathedral Grove and Kent Memorial.

FLOWERING June–July

ILYA KATSNELSON

Coast Redwood

CUPRESSACEAE

Sequoia sempervirens

Cypress Family

Preservation of the grove of redwood trees was the reason Muir Woods was designated a National Monument by President Theodore Roosevelt in 1908. Coast redwoods are found naturally in a narrow strip of land near the Pacific Ocean in California and southwestern Oregon, where heavy rains, dense fogs, and cool temperatures are favorable to their growth. Redwood trees are very long-lived, up to an estimated age of over 2,000 years, and are highly resistant to attacks by disease and insects. The thick bark also makes the trees resistant to fire, and, if damaged by fire, new branches or sprouts from the base of the tree will form. New trees may also grow from seeds, especially on burned-over lands, and seedlings may reach heights of 66 feet (20 meters) when the young trees are only 20 years old.

Once common in suitable habitats (covering an estimated 2 million acres or 810,000 hectares), heavy logging of this tree for its valuable lumber took a heavy toll on the species. Today, remnant stands have been preserved, and timber harvests are nearly all confined to second-growth trees.

Coast Redwoods, Muir Woods

ERIC KILBY

CHLOE & TREVOR VAN LOON

Western Azalea

ERICACEAE

Rhododendron occidentale

Heath Family

The delicate design of this beautiful shrub is a sight not to be forgotten where it grows along Redwood Creek. The showy and fragrant blossoms, white to cream, sometimes pink, grace monument trails through summer months. Blossoms appear only on plants that get some sunlight while plants in deep shade do not seem to produce flowers. Although not harmful to touch, it is said that all parts of the plant are poisonous if taken internally.

FLOWERING June–August

L AND R: CRICKET RASPET

Tanoak

FAGACEAE

Notholithocarpus densiflorus

Beech Family

OTHER NAMES Tanbark-Oak

SYNONYM *Lithocarpus densiflorus*

Tanoak is a broad-leaved, evergreen tree, adapted to living in shaded conditions. Its leaves are thick and leathery, and finely hairy on their underside. The fruit is a large acorn, in the past used as food after careful preparation to reduce the high tannin conent. The name 'tanoak' refers to the tree's tannin-rich bark, used in the past for tanning leather before the use of synthetic tannins. Sadly, tanoak is one one of the species most seriously affected by the disease "sudden oak death," and its number in California are decreasing.

CRICKET RASPET

Woodbalm

LAMIACEAE

Lepechinia calycina

Mint Family

This shrubby, aromatic plant has opposite leaves with toothed edges, thin and smooth when growing in shade, thicker and rough on plants exposed to strong light. Flowers in pairs, tending to lavender and orchid shades and often purple-spotted, develop in leaf axils. Corollas are broadly tubular, irregularly 5-lobed, the lower lobe prolonged into a conspicuous lip that frequently curves upward. After flowers are gone, puffy membranous calyces become conspicuous. Sometimes called **pitcher-sage**, these flowery bushes are best observed on upper slopes.

FLOWERING April–June

THEO SUMMER

California-Laurel

LAURACEAE

Umbellularia californica

Laurel Family

OTHER NAMES California Bay

This evergreen tree is found on moist slopes and canyons of the Monument. Its ability to survice in the shade makes it a common tree under the towering redwoods. Its leaves are leathery, smooth-margined and very aromatic, with a long history of medicinal uses. However, the leaves should not be used in cooking as they are now known to contain a toxic compound. The fruit, also known as "California bay nut," resembles a tiny avocado, and was traditionally eaten, especially after being dried. Wood of this laurel is valued for use as the back or sides of acoustic guitars.

FLOWERING December–May

FRANCO FOLINI

Bluebrush

RHAMNACEAE

Ceanothus thyrsiflorus

Buckthorn Family

OTHER NAMES Blueblossom

This common evergreen shrub varies widely from a low bush to a small tree. Leaves are dark and shiny, 3-veined, and alternately arranged. Feathery sprays of pale blue flowers perfume the air with their delicate fragrance. This ornamental shrub is often grown in cultivation and is widely used as a center strip plant on divided highways in northern California. Although bluebrush is best known in the chaparral community, it is also common along upper woodland trails of Muir Woods and along the mountain road approaching the monument.

FLOWERING March–June

STEPHEN

Christmas-berry

ROSACEAE

Heteromeles arbutifolia

Rose Family

SYNONYM *Photinia arbutifolia*

This shrub, often 25 feet high, is recognized by its rich evergreen leaves, oblong in shape, leather-like in texture, and sharply toothed along margins. Large clusters of flowers develop in early summer. But it is at the holiday season that this exceedingly handsome plant comes into its own. Bright red berries ripen by Thanksgiving and hang in loose bunches, adding a vivid splash of color to hills that have by then taken on a wintry tone. Known locally as **toyon**, it is one of our most loved plants. The berries were a popular Indian food and were used by early Californians in making a pleasant drink.

FLOWERING June–July

JOHN LESZCZYNSKI

LINDSEY WISE

Wood Rose

ROSACEAE

Rosa gymnocarpa

Rose Family

OTHER NAMES Baldhip Rose

The slender stems of the wood rose, which grow from 1 to 3 feet tall, are densely clothed with an armor of straight, fine prickles. Although a cluster of 2 or 3 flowers may occasionally be found, usually a solitary blossom occurs at the tip of the stem, with few flowers blooming at the same time on any one bush. The dainty blossom is less than 1 inch in diameter and a deep rose-pink color. A red, pear-shaped fruit called a hip matures in early autumn. Occasional in shady places.

FLOWERING May–July

LIAM STEELE

Western Thimbleberry

ROSACEAE

Rubus nutkanus

Rose Family

SYNONYM *Rubus parviflorus*

The tall (3 to 6 feet) slender stems of thimbleberry grow in thickets distinguished by their delicate light-green foliage. The leaves are shaped somewhat like a maple leaf, 5-lobed, 4 to 8 inches wide, with a texture like fine wool. The 5 ruffled petals of the flower, 1 to 2 inches across, bring to mind a fluffy ballet skirt. Edible pale red berries are hollow inside, their thimble shape giving to the plant its common name. Fine stands of thimbleberry may be seen in the visitor center area.

FLOWERING March–August

California Blackberry

ROSACEAE

Rubus ursinus

Rose Family

OTHER NAMES Trailing Blackberry

SYNONYM *Rubus vitifolius*

Sometimes growing erect, often with vines weak and trailing, this plant makes formidable thickets well-armed with slender prickles against those who would gather its delicious fruit. Compound leaves are 3-foliate, these, too, densely clothed with sharp prickles, and with margins coarsely toothed. Flowers are about 1 inch across and are soon replaced with fruits that ripen into sweet, juicy, black berries. Large thickets of blackberries occur near the entrance gate.

FLOWERING March–July

ABOVE Flowers
UPPER RIGHT Fruit
RIGHT Leaves

California Buckeye

SAPINDACEAE

Aesculus californica

Soapberry Family

The symmetrically rounded shape of the buckeye tree is a familiar sight on coastal hills. Palmately-shaped leaves begin to emerge from swollen buds as early as January, bright yellow-green at first, later becoming a rich dark shade. By May, long showy spikes of white to pink flowers develop. Leaves fall early, revealing pear-shaped fruits. The flower nectar is poisonous to bees. Early Indians ground the seeds and used the toxic substance to stupefy fish and bring them to the surface of pools and streams.

FLOWERING May–July

JUSTIN PAULIN

Oregon Oxalis

ABOVE Leaves
UPPER RIGHT Stem detail
RIGHT Flowers

Poison-hemlock

APIACEAE

Conium maculatum

Carrot Family

Although outwardly attractive, this rank, disagreeable weed is a regrettable addition to the assemblage of plants in Muir Woods. The erect, smooth, much-branched stems reach heights of 10 to 12 feet and are covered with irregular purple blotches. Leaves are fernlike, and the tiny flowers are in flat clusters that have a somewhat lacy pattern. Introduced from Europe, this widely naturalized weed is **extremely poisonous** (the death drink of Socrates was made from the root of poison-hemlock). It is especially abundant in the tangled growth near the entrance gate.

FLOWERING May–July

HUBERT SZCZYGIEŁ

Cow-parsnip

APIACEAE

Heracleum maximum

Carrot Family

SYNONYM *Heracleum lanatum*

Whether silhouetted against an open sky or gracing the banks of a tumbling stream, the handsome cow-parsnip is a dramatic plant of mountains and coastal hills in California. Stout branching stems grow to 12 feet in height and support large compound leaves 8 to 20 inches wide. Densely packed tiny flowers form umbrellalike heads 6 to 10 inches across. Fruits with attractive markings are a study in design. Named for the Greek god Hercules who was supposed to have used it medicinally, cow-parsnip is found in open areas where soils are moist.

FLOWERING May–July

GIANTCICADA

Sweet Cicely

APIACEAE

Osmorhiza berteroi

Carrot Family

SYNONYM *Osmorhiza chilensis*

California is in a climatic belt similar to that of Chile, South America. This has resulted in a common bond between many of our western plants and those of Chile. The former specific name chilensis places sweet cicely in this interesting group of plants common to both areas. Slender stems are 1 to 2 feet tall with deeply toothed compound leaves in 3 parts. The clusters of small flowers are arranged in an umbellate (umbrella-like) pattern. The common name refers to the thick, aromatic roots.

FLOWERING April–June

WENDY HERNIMAN

California Spikenard — ARALIACEAE

Aralia californica — Ginseng Family

This stunning plant, also known locally as **elk-clover**, lines the banks of Redwood Creek and other canyons in the Monument where soils are moist. Reaching heights of 10 feet or more, the stems, for all their stout appearance, bend and break easily. Petioles (leaf stems) of the large compound leaves are often a foot long. The ball-like dense clusters of small flowers are in an umbellate pattern at the ends of branching stems. These later develop into attractive clusters of red to purplish-black berries.

FLOWERING June–September

False Solomon's-Seal

ASPARAGACEAE

Maianthemum amplexicaule

Asparagus Family

OTHER NAMES Western Solomon's Plume

SYNONYM *Smilacina amplexicaulis*

The feathery plumes of False Solomon's-Seal have a graceful drooping habit that reveals the equally handsome foliage to best advantage. Parallel-veined leaves clasp the stem alternately and are usually 3 to 5 inches long, but sometimes reach lengths of 9 or 10 inches. The tiny crowded flowers of early spring are replaced in mid-summer by bright red berries often sprinkled with purplish dots. It may be found along all shaded trails. With it is often found **Starry False Solomon's-Seal** (*Maianthemum stellatum*), a more slender plant with an open panicle of star-shaped flowers.

FLOWERING April–June

LJ MOORE-MCCLELLAND

American Trailplant ASTERACEAE

Adenocaulon bicolor Sunflower Family

Leaves at the base of the plant, described by the specific name bicolor, are green above, white and woolly beneath. Slender flowering stems 1 to 3 feet tall are thickly covered with tiny glands, described by the generic name *Adenocaulon,* which means gland-stem; the common name 'trailplant' refers to the white underside of the leaf which is easily turned over when hiking, providing signs of a passing hiker. Clusters of inconspicuous flowers appear in summer. *Adenocaulon* is found along Monument trails where there is shade.

FLOWERING May–August

JOHN DREW

Sweet Coltsfoot

ASTERACEAE

Petasites frigidus

Sunflower Family

SYNONYM *Petasites palmatus*

The feature that attracts the visitor to this plant is the remarkable leaves. Palmately shaped and deeply lobed and veined, they are green above and covered with white woolly hairs beneath. Leaves continue to increase in size from their first appearance in early spring to mid-summer when they are commonly 12 to 16 inches broad. Flower stems are 12 to 20 inches tall, each crowned with a flat dense cluster of whitish flowers. Coltsfoot may be found along Redwood Creek and in moist canyons. A fine stand may be seen near headquarters.

FLOWERING March–April

ROGER RAICHE

California Toothwort

BRASSICACEAE

Cardamine californica

Mustard Family

SYNONYM *Dentaria californica*

Early in January toothworts begin to shine through the dark woods with their glisteny-white blossoms. The plant is 10 to 14 inches tall with two kinds of leaves: those on upper stems have deeply cut pointed lobes with toothed margins, while those on lower stems are rounded. The undersides of leaves are often purple. Branched stems are several-flowered, these white at first, often later tinged with pink. The four petals are lifted and spread in fair weather, or folded and hanging down like bells in rain, heavy fog, or at night. Other common names include **milkmaids** and **rainbells**.

FLOWERING January–June

KEN-ICHI UEDA

Western Morning-Glory

CONVOLVULACEAE

Calystegia occidentalis

Morning-Glory Family

OTHER NAMES Chaparral False Bindweed

SYNONYM *Convolvulus occidentalis*

The woody stems of this attractive perennial vine climb over shrubs or trail on the ground in open places, a common sight on canyon slopes. The bases of the alternate, sharply triangular leaves are marked by long pointed lobes (hastate). The broad, funnel-shaped corollas, ribbed where petals join, are numerous along the length of the trailing stem, white or pinkish in color, often becoming purplish with age. *Convolvulus,* the former generic name, is from a Latin word meaning to entwine, and this plant entwines its host many times. Look for it on upper trails and along the entrance road.

FLOWERING May–July

Coastal Manroot

CUCURBITACEAE

Marah oregana

Gourd Family

The graceful trailing vines clambering over stumps and low shrubs give no hint of the huge root that lies beneath the ground; the root as large as a man's body leads to the common name of manroot. Handsome leaves up to 8 inches across are ivy-shaped, sometimes deeply lobed. Creamy-white flowers are roundish, 5-lobed, and about ½ inch across. Two species are found in Muir Woods. Fruits of both resemble a roundish cucumber, this one sparsely covered with weak spines, those of *Marah fabacea* with dense stiff spines.

FLOWERING March–June

NOLAN EXE

Modesty

HYDRANGEACEAE

Whipplea modesta Hydrangea Family

Cascading down a shaded bank or creeping over other plants, the long trailing stems of modesty with showers of small white blossoms were formerly a charming addition to the flora of Muir Woods; however, this plant is reported as no longer present in the Monument by the Park Service. Modesty is known from Marin County and northern California, northward into western Oregon. The short-stemmed, oval-shaped leaves are opposite and usually less than an inch long. The flowers that occur in clusters at the tips of stems are delicately fragrant and make a showy display when in full bloom.

FLOWERING March–June

MATT BERGER

Yerba Buena

LAMIACEAE

Clinopodium douglasii

Mint Family

SYNONYM *Satureja douglasii*

Its delicate aromatic scent often marks this modest member of the mint family before it is seen. Small roundish, evergreen leaves, oppositely arranged, have gently scalloped margins. Tubular-shaped flowers about ¼ inch long develop in upper leaf axils. Long ago this charming plant grew profusely in San Francisco, and for a time the name Yerba Buena was attached to that early settlement. Equally familiar to Indians and mission fathers, it was valued for its medicinal uses. Yerba buena means "good herb." It is common in Muir Woods in partially shaded places.

FLOWERING May–June

RYAN DURAND

Large-Flower Fairybells — LILIACEAE

Prosartes smithii — Lily Family

SYNONYM *Disporum smithi*

This leafy perennial hides its flowers so well that a season may come and go without discovering them. Plants are often 2 feet high with alternate, parallel-veined leaves. At the ends of branching stems, 1 to 5 cylindrical-shaped creamy or greenish-white flowers hang on slender stalks beneath terminal leaves. By summer, scarlet berries appear, as attractive in turn as the flowers. Blooming at the same time and often in the same place is the similar *Disporum hookeri*, called fairy lanterns. Flowers are greenish-white with the segments spreading so that stamens are more readily noticed.

FLOWERING March–May

HENRIK KIBAK

Common Starlily

MELANTHIACEAE

Toxicoscordion fremontii

False Hellebore Family

SYNONYM *Zigadenus fremontii*

In places exposed to sunlight these sturdy plants grow from 1 to 3 feet tall. The basal leaves are narrow, parallel-veined, and shorter than the flowering stem. Greenish-white, star-shaped flowers are closely clustered in a pyramidal pattern, the entire inflorescence often measuring several inches in length. This handsome plant is common in both the forest and on the shrubby slopes above the Monument. Some members of this genus are poisonous to grazing animals, and at least one species is known as death-camas.

FLOWERING March–June

GAIL

Pacific Trillium

MELANTHIACEAE

Trillium ovatum

False Hellebore Family

Affectionately called **wake-robin** by those who know it well, spring has truly arrived by the time this plant makes its appearance on the steep slopes of Muir Woods. A single flower nodding on a slender stem is accented by 3 large dark green leaves that grow in a whorl from the top of the main stalk. The pure white corolla turns to pink and rose as the flower ages. **Giant green trillium** (*Trillium chloropetalum*) is also found occasionally in the Monument, differing from the wake-robin by a larger, dark red flower arising directly without a flower stem from the whorl of leaves.

FLOWERING March–April

CLAUDE KOLWELTER

Miner's-lettuce

MONTIACEAE

Claytonia perfoliata

Candy-Flower Family

SYNONYM *Montia perfoliata*

The flowering stems of miner's-lettuce appear to force their way directly through the conspicuous saucer-shaped pair of united leaves that develop high on an otherwise naked stem. The entire plant may be 3 to 12 inches tall and leaves may vary from long and narrow to triangular shaped. The flowers are about ¼ inch across and often have a pinkish tinge. California Indians used the plant for food. They placed the herbage at the entrance of red ant nests where the insects in crawling over stems and leaves imparted a natural vinegar taste to the salad greens.

FLOWERING March–July

LAURA GAUDETTE

Western Baneberry

RANUNCULACEAE

Actaea rubra

Buttercup Family

SYNONYM *Actaea arguta*

A plant of shady, moist places, baneberry has sturdy stems 12 to 20 inches tall which support spreading compound leaves sharply toothed along their margins. Flowers are in terminal clusters with petals shorter than. the numerous stamens. Much more conspicuous and attractive than the flowers are the bright red berries that develop late in summer. These fruits are poisonous. Although scarce in Muir Woods, a few plants may be found near the headquarters and along the main trails.

FLOWERING May–July

DEE HIMES

Oregon Anemone

RANUNCULACEAE

Anemonoides oregana

Buttercup Family

SYNONYM *Anemone oregana*

The slender-stemmed anemone, 4 to 12 inches tall, contributes to the delicate undergrowth flora in Muir Woods. A whorl of 3 compound leaves, these again in 3's, develops just below the flowering stem. Look closely at the lavender-tinged blossom—there are no petals, but instead the sepals that usually enfold the petals here become the showy structure that we call the flower. The generic name *Anemone* is from a Greek word that refers to wind movement, and anemones as a group are often called windflowers.

FLOWERING April–May

OLEG KOSTERIN

ABOVE Leaves, fruit
RIGHT Flowers

Woodland Strawberry

ROSACEAE

Fragaria vesca

Rose Family

SYNONYM *Fragaria californica*

The rose family provides many edible fruits which include the popular wild strawberry, the source of our domestic hybrids. Three leaflets form a compound leaf and runners root at nodes to start new plants. In Muir Woods, mature fruit is rare and scarcely justifies the abundance of blossoms to be seen earlier in the season. The genus name is from a Latin word *fragum* meaning fragrant, and this is exactly the word to describe the ripened fruit when found.

FLOWERING February–June

KEN-ICHI UEDA

Fragrant Bedstraw

RUBIACEAE

Galium triflorum

Madder Family

Bedstraws, of which there are several in Muir Woods, may be recognized by their square stems and whorled leaf pattern. The plant shown here has little hooks on the underside that enable long, weak, often reclining stems to clamber successfully over other plants. Leaves are in whorls of 6. Flowers are tiny, greenish-white, inconspicuous, and develop later into a two-parted fruit densely covered with long, hooked bristles. Herbage is sweetly fragrant. Bedstraw grows along all Monument trails.

FLOWERING May–July

Crevice Alumroot

SAXIFRAGACEAE

Heuchera micrantha

Saxifrage Family

The handsome leaves of this decorative plant are rounded, shallowly lobed, and in a thick basal cluster. Naked flowering stems grow 1 to 2 feet tall, branching into delicate, lacy, open panicles of tiny flowers that bend gracefully over a moist mossy bank against their own background of spreading leaves. Although not abundant in the Monument, alumroot is one of the beautiful sights along Muir Woods trails, especially common on the banks of Redwood Creek near the entrance gate.

FLOWERING May–July.

P. HOLROYD

Woodland-Star

SAXIFRAGACEAE

Lithophragma affine

Saxifrage Family

From a basal cluster of rounded leaves with long petioles, flowering stems grow from 8 to 20 inches tall and are covered with tiny glandlike hairs. Delicate pure white flowers are closely attached to the stem. The petals are deeply lobed and fringed, giving the appearance of an irregular 5-pointed star. Woodland-Star is easily overlooked because of its fragile form, but it may be found on mossy banks where shade and moisture linger.

FLOWERING February–May

BEE TOGETHER

Stinging Nettle

URTICACEAE

Urtica dioica

Nettle Family

SYNONYM *Urtica californica*

One of our more robust herbaceous plants, nettles often grow to 6 feet in height. Broad oval-shaped leaves are opposite and dark green in color. Feathery flower clusters develop at each leaf joint for almost the entire length of the tall plant stem. The tiny greenish-white flowers have no petals. There is no hint of the stinging hairs that cover all parts of the plant. The gentlest contact with these poison-filled hairs often inflicts a wound on the unwary that may cause pain for several days. Nettles grow along many trails and are especially common near the park entrance gate.

FLOWERING April–July

ABOVE Cutleaf Burnweed
RIGHT Coastal Burnweed

Cutleaf Burnweed

ASTERACEAE

Senecio glomeratus

Sunflower Family

SYNONYM *Erechtites arguta*

Burnweed is a traveler that has crossed the ocean from Australia and New Zealand to become naturalized in a strange land far from home. A robust plant often 6 feet tall, the silvery-green leaves are deeply cut with margins irregularly toothed. Yellow disk flowers are arranged in loose clusters. A similar plant (also introduced), **Coastal Burnweed** (*Senecio minimus*), differs by having dentate leaves not at all lobed, and flower clusters usually broader, more numerous, and pale yellow or cream-colored. Both are weedy, and in Muir Woods effort is being made to eradicate these foreign plants.

FLOWERING June–August

Leopard Lily

LILIACEAE

Lilium pardalinum

Lily Family

This decorative lily grows in Muir Woods as an occasional single plant, or 2 or 3 together, a dramatic trailside addition in wet, springy places. A stout stem grows from 2 to 4 feet tall and supports several whorls of long narrow leaves. Nodding flowers vary from light to deep orange-red, the segments conspicuously marked with large purple spots. The first scientific collection of leopard lily was made in the "vicinity of San Francisco" and could well have been along these trails.

FLOWERING May–July

JOHN BARKLA

California-poppy

PAPAVERACEAE

Eschscholzia californica

Poppy Family

Although California poppies are at their best in open sunny places, the satin petals shine and shimmer in many different habitats. Were it not for the exquisite beauty of the blossom, the interesting and much dissected leaves would win more attention. Fragile though it appears, the plant is nevertheless utilitarian as well. Indians, after special treatment in cooking, used the leaves and stems as greens; a drug made from the plant is still used medicinally as a remedy for headache. In Muir Woods, poppies are found on upper trails and in open places.

FLOWERING February–September

CRICKET RASPET

Bush Monkeyflower

PHRYMACEAE

Diplacus aurantiacus

Lopseed Family

SYNONYM *Mimulus aurantiacus*

Monkeyflowers are among our most appealing, yet most variable, wild plants. They include dwarf members 1 inch tall to sturdy bushes represented by the handsome plant pictured here. Bush monkeyflower, its erect much-branched stems profusely covered with bright yellow-orange blossoms, grows from 2 to 4 feet tall. Dark green slender leaves are opposite, serrate along the edges, and often sticky. The corolla is tubular, narrow where it is encased in the long calyx, gradually enlarged into the flaring outer lobes. This ornamental plant adds a warm splash of color to upper trails.

FLOWERING April–August

CRICKET RASPET

California Buttercup

RANUNCULACEAE

Ranunculus californicus

Buttercup Family

This slender-stemmed, branching plant may be 10 to 30 inches tall. Deeply cut leaves are on long stems mostly from the base of the plant. The shining waxy petals form a golden saucer up to ¾ inch across in which are nestled numerous golden stamens. The scientific name Ranunculus means "little frog" and refers to the damp habitat in which both frogs and many kinds of buttercups are found. For this reason, look for this buttercup where soil is moist.

FLOWERING February–June

JOHN LESZCZYNSKI

Redwood Violet

VIOLACEAE

Viola sempervirens

Violet Family

The ground-cover plants are one of the attractive features of the redwood forest due to the fact that so many of them are evergreen throughout the year. The redwood violet belongs to this group, its small roundish leaves covering large areas in an open matlike pattern. Short-stemmed (2 to 4 inches long) lemon-yellow violets appear in early spring, the 3 lower petals delicately lined with purple veins. Common along the main trails that border Redwood Creek.

FLOWERING April–May

RAPPMAN

Rigid Betony

LAMIACEAE

Stachys rigida

Mint Family

ALSO CALLED Rough Hedgenettle

Betony is a member of the mint family, which is usually marked by 4-angled stems, opposite leaves, and an aromatic scent. With leaves similar to stinging nettle (also in Muir Woods, see page 52), and because it often grows along hedgerows, it is commonly called hedge-nettle. Simple, erect stems 1 to 3 feet tall often branch into several flowering stalks. These support crowded whorls of cylindrical, rose-purple flowers, the upper lobe erect and the lower lip flaring. Betony is abundant along all Muir Woods trails.

FLOWERING June–August

ALAN ROCKEFELLER

ALEX BARNARD

Bluebead-Lily

LILIACEAE

Clintonia andrewsiana

Lily Family

ALSO CALLED Andrew's Clintonia

Glossy, rich green leaves, often as much as 10 inches long and 4 inches wide, are arranged in a symmetrically circular pattern close to the ground. A single stem grows to a height of 15 to 20 inches and bears a cluster of rose-red bells on its summit. These are followed by large, dark blue berries which remind one of delicate porcelain. By summer, deer have altered the distinctive leaf arrangement by a pattern of half-nibbled leaves, for they consider this one of the tasty plants of the forest. Bluebead-Lily is common along many trails.

FLOWERING May–July

CALEB CATTO

Striped Coralroot

ORCHIDACEAE

Corallorhiza striata

Orchid Family

Coralroot belongs to a group of plants called **saprophytes** which have no green color in stems or leaves to indicate the presence of chlorophyll, a necessary ingredient for the manufacture of food. This plant lives on organic material provided by decaying twigs, leaves, and logs that make up the humus on the forest floor. A plant 10 to 15 inches tall, it is named for its coral-shaped root system. A closely related species, ***Corallorhiza maculata***, also occurs in the monument. Both are rare in Muir Woods but may be found occasionally in shady places on steep canyon slopes.

FLOWERING April–June

FRANCO FOLINI

Franciscan Paintbrush

OROBANCHACEAE

Castilleja subinclusa var. ***franciscana***

Broom-Rape Family

SYNONYM *Castilleja franciscana*

The scarlet tufts of Franciscan Paintbrush add a brilliant splash of color to the frequently subdued aspect of the woods. With corollas relatively inconspicuous, it is the calyces and bracts which enfold the inner flower parts that provide the showy color of this popular plant. Paintbrushes are often parasitic on other plants. Why this should be so is something of a mystery for, unlike many parasites, they have both chlorophyll for photosynthesis and adequate root systems for the intake of water and minerals. Several species grow in the Monument, mostly on upper trails.

FLOWERING April–June

ALAN ROCKEFELLER

Indian-Warrior

OROBANCHACEAE

Pedicularis densiflora

Broom-Rape Family

ALSO CALLED Warrior's Plume

The thick clusters of fern like leaves first attract attention to this plant. Several flowering stems 5 to 20 inches tall stand erectly above these finely-cut, mostly basal leaves, making an altogether handsome plant. Deep purple-red flowers are in a dense spike, somewhat similar to the closely related paintbrush. Colonies of Indian-warrior often make showy displays where filtered sunlight warms the soil. Legend tells us that each plant marks the spot of a fallen Indian warrior of long ago.

FLOWERING January–June

Oregon Oxalis

OXALIDACEAE

Oxalis oregana

Wood-Sorrel Family

Also commonly known as **redwood-sorrel**, this widespread plant is not even remotely related to the clovers which its leaves so closely resemble. Spreading by underground stems, it often carpets large areas of the forest floor. The evergreen leaves fold tightly back in direct sunlight, a habit that protects this shade plant from losing too much moisture. As the sun and shade shift places, the leaves may respond by folding and opening several times a day. Flowers less than an inch across are mostly pink, sometimes white or deep rose; however while an abundant plant growing at the base of the redwoods, only a few plants will produce flowers.

FLOWERING February–September

VELODROME

Crimson Monkeyflower

PHRYMACEAE

Erythranthe cardinalis

Lopseed Family

SYNONYM *Mimulus cardinalis*

In a large and variable genus, Crimson Monkeyflower is indeed a stunning representative. Branched stems 1 to 2½ feet tall support opposite leaves with toothed margins, both stems and leaves clothed with long soft hairs. The yellowish throat of the corolla is held tightly by a tubular calyx, then flares into spreading, irregular lobes, with the four stamens conspicuously arched against the upper lip. Look for this handsome plant along stream banks or springy places where soil is deep and moist.

FLOWERING April–October

MY-LAN LE

Western Starflower

PRIMULACEAE

Lysimachia latifolia

Primrose Family

SYNONYM *Trientalis latifolia*

By early summer dainty starflowers abundantly dot the forest floor like sparkling pink jewels. A whorl of leaves, not unlike those of trillium but of a thinner texture and rarely limited to 3 as in trillium, mark the plant long before the slender flower stems develop. Flowers are pale to deep pink, sometimes edged with white, the corolla spreading almost flat. Starflower adds a delicate and charming note to the flora of Muir Woods.

FLOWERING May–July

KEN-ICHI UEDA

Henderson's Shootingstar

PRIMULACEAE

Primula hendersonii

Primrose Family

SYNONYM *Dodecatheon hendersoni*

From a basal cluster of spatula-shaped leaves, the red stems of shootingstar grow 10 to 15 inches tall. These bear at their summits a crown of delicately perfumed, magenta-colored blossoms. The 5 petals are swept backward like a coronet. The dark purplish-black stamens thus exposed are united and come to a slender point, giving to the plant another common name, bird-bill. Rarely growing in large masses, as do their mountain cousins, shootingstars are scattered intermittently along higher monument trails.

FLOWERING February–May

DON LOARIE

Fragrant Fringecup

SAXIFRAGACEAE

Tellima grandiflora

Saxifrage Family

Fringecups are a delightful addition to the early spring parade of flowers. Both basal and stem leaves are present, somewhat roundish in shape and shallowly toothed along the margins. Simple flowering stems 1 to 2 feet tall support numerous bell-shaped blossoms along their lengths. The corolla is about ¼ inch across, greenish-white in color, and has a fringed margin that is often reddish. This plant is the only representative of the genus *Tellima* and is found in western states along the Pacific Coast. In Muir Woods it grows in moist, shady places.

FLOWERING April–June

GWYN WILLIAMS

California Beeplant

SCROPHULARIACEAE

Scrophularia californica

Figwort Family

Often ignored because of its rank and weedy habit, this sturdy plant has 4-angled stems, 3 to 5 feet tall, which support large, coarse, opposite leaves somewhat triangular in shape and toothed along the margins. The inconspicuous flowers are ¼ to ½ inch in length and reddish-brown in color. A nectar disk occurs at the base of each flower, making this a favorite plant of honeybees (and hummingbirds). The genus was named long ago when certain species were successful in curing the dread disease scrofula. It grows in open places along Redwood Creek.

FLOWERING February–July.

ABOVE Basal rosette of leaves
RIGHT Flower

MURRAY DAWSON

PETER NEISH

Bull Thistle

ASTERACEAE

Cirsium vulgare

Sunflower Family

This common and aggressive weed of hills and valleys has invaded the shady habitat of Muir Woods. From a basal rosette of coarsely toothed leaves, a single branching stem grows 2 to 4 feet tall, leaves becoming fewer on upper parts of the plant. Both stems and leaves are armed with savage spines. The typical thistle flowers are purple, sometimes pale lavender. A native of Europe, it is found along Monument trails, although ongoing efforts are being made to eradicate it.

FLOWERING June–September

CRICKET RASPET

Pacific Hound's-tongue

BORAGINACEAE

Adelinia grande

Borage Family

SYNONYM *Cynoglossum grande*

Hound's-tongue grows as a rank, coarse plant, 1 to 3 feet tall, on well-drained, shaded slopes. The common name, a translation of the generic name *Cynoglossum,* refers to the shape and texture of the basal leaves. The intensely blue flowers are in loose clusters at the ends of long stems, and remind one of woodland forget-me-nots, to which they are closely related. Fruits consist of tiny nutlets with numerous hooks that cling to animal fur and human clothing and thus are carried to far places, there to perpetuate the plant in new locations.

FLOWERING March–June

CRICKET RASPET

Woodland Forget-me-not

BORAGINACEAE

Myosotis latifolia

Borage Family

This well-known horticultural plant recalls to native Marin County residents an inn that once stood at the upper end of Muir Woods before it was a monument. From the garden of that old hotel, which marked the end of a spur of the historic Mt. Tamalpais and Muir Woods Railroad, both long since gone, this one plant escaped and spread to many parts of the woods, its light blue flowers appearing in the most unlikely places. A popular garden addition, among its native companions here it must be considered a weed and its continued growth in Muir Woods is not encouraged.

FLOWERING May–July

HENRIK KIBAK

Douglas Iris

IRIDACEAE

Iris douglasiana

Iris Family

Iris, a Greek word meaning rainbow, alludes to the wide range of shades exhibited by flowers of this group. The Douglas Iris runs a color gamut from deep purple and lilac to shades of lavender and creamy-white. Stems are 12 to 20 inches tall, somewhat flattened, sometimes with side branches, each stem crowned with 2 or 3 blossoms. To find even one of these aristocratic plants in bloom would make any walk worthwhile, but nature with extravagant abandon has made this one of the common and abundant plants of spring, and the tall stately iris is found along all trails.

FLOWERING April–June

CRICKET RASPET

Western Blue-Eyed-Grass

IRIDACEAE

Sisyrinchium bellum

Iris Family

Closely related to the iris, this modest member of the same family is a delightful addition to the flora of Muir Woods. Slender grasslike leaves are usually shorter than the erect flowering stem which grows 10 to 20 inches tall. The purple-blue corollas are enhanced by bright yellow centers and 3 united golden stamens. Blue-eyed-grass was known to early Californians for its medicinal properties. A tea made from the plant was used as a remedy for reducing fever. This charming plant grows in filtered sunlight and open places of upper trails.

FLOWERING March–May

ABOVE Leaves
RIGHT Flower

Western Wild Ginger

ARISTOLOCHIACEAE

Asarum caudatum

Birthwort Family

The long-stemmed, heart-shaped, evergreen leaves of wild ginger are deeply veined. They often form a solid carpet in shady places wherever soil is moist and deep. With petals absent, the calyx, with its 3 lobes developed into long (1 to 3 inches) slender appendages, forms the brown flower that lies almost on the ground beneath its canopy of rich green leaves. The stems and roots are spicily aromatic, giving to the plant its common name. Large patches of *Asarum* may be seen throughout the Monument and particularly along Redwood Creek trails.

FLOWERING February–June

ABOVE Flowers
LEFT Fruit

Checker Fritillary

LILIACEAE

Fritillaria affinis

Lily Family

SYNONYM *Fritillaria lanceolata*

Known by many common names which include mission bells, bronze bells, and checkerlily, this charming but retiring plant cccurs sparingly in Muir Woods. Slender lance-shaped leaves are in several whorls on stems 1 to 2 feet tall. Flowers, 1 to 1½ inches long, mottled, dull green to brown in color, hang like bells along the erect or curving stem. The fruit is a curiously winged capsule containing numerous seeds in neatly divided sections, a seed vessel as interesting and attractive as the flower. Fritillaries may be found occasionally on upper trails.

FLOWERING February–May

CRICKET RASPET

Fetid Adder's-Tongue

LILIACEAE

Scoliopus bigelovii

Lily Family

The slender stems of *Scoliopus*, 3 to 6 inches long, appear in mid-December. They support terminal blossoms with flower parts arranged in 2 series: the conspicuous outer parts (3 sepals) are greenish, delicately veined with fine reddish-brown lines; the erect inner parts (3 petals) are extremely narrow and brownish in color, the entire blossom about 1 inch across and perfectly camouflaged against the forest floor. Two leaves (rarely more) develop later and, mottled with dark blotches, are a conspicuous feature long after flowers are gone. For all its delicate beauty, the flower has an offensive odor.

FLOWERING December–February

ABOVE Western Swordfern (*Polystichum minutum*)

Many visitors consider the ferns of Muir Woods the most delightful attraction in the Monument. At certain seasons they are indeed the most conspicuous feature of the undergrowth, and at all seasons they add a cool evergreen note to the general aspect of the woods. Currently, fourteen species of fern are known from the Monument, twelve of which are illustrated on the following pages.

Ferns have no flowers and produce no seeds. They belong to a plant group that reproduces by spores. Botanically they are considered a more primitive group than the flowering plants. Look on the back of a mature fern leaf (frond). One will see powdery-appearing fruit-dots usually arranged in distinctive patterns. These are the *sori* containing spore cases (*sporangia*), in which spores develop and mature. These spores, however, reproduce not a fern but a small, inconspicuous 'inbetween plant' called a *prothallus*. In wet winter months a careful search of the ground beneath a fern often reveals these tiny plants. The prothallus produces the male and female structures that in turn yield another fern like the parent plant. This "alternation of generations" is indeed one of nature's wonders.

DAN MACNEAL

Western Ladyfern

ATHYRIACEAE

Athyrium cyclosorum

Lady Fern Family

SYNONYM *Athyrium filix-femina* subsp. *cyclosorum*

The lovely ladyfern is one of the most conspicuous ferns in Muir Woods. The broad, lohg, lacy fronds grace the banks of Redwood Creek and contribute in large measure to the cool green aspect of the woods. The fronds are annual, dying back in winter. Tightly rolled fiddlenecks begin to show in late spring and by midsummer these develop into fronds 2 to 5 feet long and as much as 12 inches wide, arching in a graceful pattern from a central crown. The pinnae are deeply fringed and the sorus-pattern on the underside is crescent-shaped.

Giant Chainfern

BLECHNACEAE

Woodwardia fimbriata

Chain Fern Family

The regular and uniform pattern of the coarse fronds of this large plant distinguish it at once from other ferns. From a woody crown, fronds 3 to 6 feet long and 12 to 20 inches wide stand erect, or the lower ones often curving. The common name comes from the sorus-pattern on the blade underside which resembles long links of a chain. Once an abundant plant

ABOVE Chain-like sori on underside of frond

of our coastal forests, it has been much-depleted by the gathering of the handsome fronds for decorative purposes. It may be seen in the vicinity of Cathedral Grove.

TOM SCAVO

Bracken Fern

DENNSTAEDTIACEAE

Pteridium aquilinum

Bracken Fern Family

The common and widespread braken fern thrives in shaded forest, woodland, and on open hillsides. Stems 1 to 4 feet tall may be erect or reclining. A deciduous fern, tightly rolled new shoots begin to show in February and by summer the much-branched, coarse, broad fronds grow singly or in large tangled patches. Spores develop along margins of leaves and become conspicuous with maturity. Although the fresh young shoots are considered poisonous, northern California Indians ate them after special cooking. The broad fronds were used by early settlers for thatching cabin roofs.

PETER BRASTOW

Coast Woodfern

DRYOPTERIDACEAE

Dryopteris arguta

Wood Fern Family

This attractive fern is found on well-drained slopes of forest and woodland. The fronds, 1 to 2½ feet long, arise from a woody root system and stand erect in a somewhat sparse and asymmetrical pattern. With a lacy appearance somewhat similar to the ladyfern, woodfern may be separated by the different habitat, by the sorus-pattern which in the wood fern is round, and by the fact that the woodfern is an evergreen whereas the ladyfern dies back in winter.

MY-LAN LE

Western Swordfern

DRYOPTERIDACEAE

Polystichum munitum

Wood Fern Family

The handsome evergreen swordfern makes such a familiar pattern it could well be considered the hallmark of Muir Woods. The coarse but attractive fronds 2 to 5 feet long emerge in a profuse fashion from a central woody crown, and stand rigidly erect or gracefully recurved. Where each pinna is attached to the midrib, there is a projection that resembles the hilt of a sword. From this relatively broad "hilt" the leaflet tapers to a sharp point, the entire structure like a miniature sword. The related **Dudley's Swordfern** (*Polystichum dudleyi*) is also known from the Monument. It has arching frons to about 3 feet long, and its pinnae are typically deeply lobed.

Western Swordfern

Dudley's Swordfern

BOGSUCKERS

Giant Horsetail

EQUISETACEAE

Equisetum telmateia

Horsetail Family

Closely related to the 'true ferns', this remarkable plant is numbered among our most ancient and primitive members of the plant kingdom. In the Carbon Age of geology, when coal fields were being formed, Equisetum grew as a forest tree 50 to 100 feet tall. Like the ferns, it reproduces by spores. These are borne on a conelike structure at the tips of special stems. The luxurious growth of the vegetative stem is easily mistaken for leaves but is in reality branches. *Equisetum* has the peculiar ability to store silica in its stems and branches, giving the plant a sandpapery texture. Used by the pioneers to scour cooking utensils, the name **scouring rush** still clings as a common name.

California Polypody

POLYPODIACEAE

Polypodium californicum

Polypody Family

The polypody ferns are easily recognizable by the interesting manner in which the pinnae seem to flow into the midrib, never quite coming to a clean-cut end. The California polypody is distinguished by the comparatively stubby tips of leaf-segments. Stems are straw-colored, 4 to 20 inches long. The sori on the underside appear as large, brown, velvety dots arranged along either side of the midvein. Indians made an extract from the roots as a treatment for sore eyes. Look for this polypody in rocky soil of steep banks in wet months of spring.

RYAN DURAND

Licorice Fern

POLYPODIACEAE

Polypodium glycyrrhiza

Polypody Family

Rarely found growing directly on the ground, the licorice fern is an epiphytic plant that is commonly found on mossy fallen logs, moist mossy tree trunks, or rocks along streams where they are kept wet with spray. It is similar to the California polypody but the fronds are usually longer (10 to 25 inches) and the segments have slender elongated tips. The root of this fern smells like licorice when fresh, hence the common name. Dependent upon moisture, the fronds are often withered and dried by mid-July.

Leather Fern

POLYPODIACEAE

Polypodium scouleri

Polypody Family

Although numbered among the more interesting members of the fern family, leather fern occurs but sparingly in Muir Woods. The few fronds grow 6 to 20 inches long. The sori, in the characteristic pattern of the polypody group, form large circular disks on the underside and are usually found only on the upper frond segments, crowded against the midrib. The common name comes from the texture of the leaves, which are thick and leathery. A few handsome plants grow on fallen tree trunks high above main trails.

GWYN WILLIAMS

Western Maidenhair Fern

PTERIDACEAE

Adiantum aleuticum

Maidenhair Fern Family

Closely related to the California maidenhair (next page), but not so delicate, is the stunning *Adiantum aleuticum* or 'fivefinger fern'. The palm-shaped fronds with fingers widespread arise from a scaly base on stems sometimes 2 feet tall. The leaflets are coarser and closer together than the maidenhair in an almost crowded pattern, the sori again inrolled on the margins. Although scarce in Muir Woods, this beautiful fern occasionally grows in thick masses along deeply cut stream channels of side canyons. The dark shiny stems were used in basket-making by California Indians.

AMELIA TAUBER

California Maidenhair Fern — PTERIDACEAE

Adiantum jordanii — Maidenhair Fern Family

Surely there is no more graceful fern than the California maidenhair. Florists recognize this and have made certain cultivated species familiar to many. Several fronds, mostly rigidly erect, but sometimes curving gently, arise from a scaly base. Polished purple-brown stems, 10 to 20 inches tall, are as attractive as the daintily fringed pinnae of the spreading fronds. Only in mature plants can the sori (fruit-dots) be detected, tightly rolled along the margins on the underside of leaflets. This maidenhair grows along moist banks and in steep side canyons.

ABOVE Upper surface of frond
RIGHT Lower surface of frond covered with sporangia

California Goldfern

PTERIDACEAE

Pentagramma triangularis

Maidenhair Fern Family

SYNONYM *Pityrogramma triangularis*

The triangle-shaped fronds of this rather small fern grow 4 to 12 inches tall in a crowded cluster from a small root crown. The underside is covered with a white to golden waxy powder, which accounts for the common name goldback fern. A charming addition to the ferns of Muir Woods, it may be found in shady, dry, often rocky places along upper trails.

Muir Woods National Monument Vascular Plant Species List

Species in **bold type** are illustrated in this book. Note that scientific names or common names are those used by the National Park Service and may differ from those used by the authors.

* = probably present in Muir Woods National Monument.

Adoxaceae

- ❏ *Sambucus nigra* ssp. *canadensis* black elderberry
- ❏ *Sambucus racemosa* var. *racemosa* red elderberry

Anacardiaceae

- ❏ ***Toxicodendron diversilobum*** Pacific poison oak, p. 10

Apiaceae

- ❏ ***Conium maculatum*** poison-hemlock, p. 30
- ❏ *Foeniculum vulgare* sweet fennel
- ❏ ***Heracleum maximum*** common cowparsnip, p. 31
- ❏ ***Osmorhiza berteroi*** sweet cicely, p. 32
- ❏ *Sanicula crassicaulis* Pacific black snakeroot

Apocynaceae

- ❏ *Vinca major* periwinkle

Araceae

- ❏ *Zantedeschia aethiopica* calla lily

Araliaceae

- ❏ ***Aralia californica*** California spikenard, p. 33
- ❏ *Hedera helix* English ivy

Aristolochiaceae

- ❏ ***Asarum caudatum*** British Columbia wildginger, p. 75

Asparagaceae

- ❏ *Brodiaea elegans* harvest brodiaea
- ❏ *Chlorogalum pomeridianum* wavyleaf soap plant
- ❏ *Dichelostemma capitatum* bluedicks
- ❏ ***Maianthemum racemosum*** false Solomon's-seal, p. 34
- ❏ *Maianthemum stellatum* little false Solomon's-seal
- ❏ *Triteleia laxa* Ithuriel's spear

Asteraceae

- ❏ *Achillea millefolium* common yarrow
- ❏ ***Adenocaulon bicolor*** American trailplant, p. 35
- ❏ *Anaphalis margaritacea* common pearlyeverlasting
- ❏ *Arctotheca calendula* capeweed
- ❏ *Artemisia californica* coastal sagebrush
- ❏ *Artemisia douglasiana* Douglas' sagewort

- ❏ *Baccharis pilularis* coyotebrush
- ❏ *Carduus pycnocephalus* Italian plumeless thistle
- ❏ *Centaurea calcitrapa* purple starthistle
- ❏ *Cirsium occidentale* var. *californicum* cobwebby thistle
- ❏ *Cirsium quercetorum* brownie thistle
- ❏ ***Cirsium vulgare*** bull thistle, p. 70
- ❏ *Cotula coronopifolia* brassbuttons
- ❏ * *Cynara cardunculus* artichoke
- ❏ * ***Erechtites glomerata*** cutleaf burnweed, p. 53
- ❏ ***Erechtites minima*** Australian coastal burnweed, p. 53
- ❏ *Eriophyllum confertiflorum* golden-yarrow
- ❏ *Eriophyllum confertiflorum* var. *confertiflorum* golden-yarrow
- ❏ *Eurybia radulina* roughleaf aster
- ❏ *Gamochaeta purpurea* purple cudweed
- ❏ *Gnaphalium palustre* cudweed
- ❏ * *Gnaphalium ramosissimum*
- ❏ *Grindelia hirsutula* bract gumweed
- ❏ *Helenium puberulum* rosilla
- ❏ *Hemizonia fasciculata* clustered tarweed
- ❏ *Hieracium albiflorum* white hawkweed
- ❏ *Hypochaeris glabra* smooth cat's ear
- ❏ *Hypochaeris radicata* common cat's-ear
- ❏ *Lactuca saligna* willow-leaf lettuce
- ❏ *Logfia gallica* narrowleaf cottonrose
- ❏ *Madia elegans* common madia
- ❏ *Madia gracilis* grassy tarweed
- ❏ *Madia sativa* Chilean tarweed
- ❏ ***Petasites frigidus* var. *palmatus*** arctic sweet-colt's-foot, p. 36
- ❏ *Picris echioides* bristly oxtongue
- ❏ *Pseudognaphalium californicum* ladies' tobacco
- ❏ *Pseudognaphalium luteoalbum* winged cudweed
- ❏ *Silybum marianum* blessed milkthistle
- ❏ *Solidago californica* California goldenrod
- ❏ *Sonchus asper* ssp. *asper* spiny sowthistle
- ❏ *Sonchus oleraceus* annual sowthistle
- ❏ *Symphyotrichum chilense* Pacific aster
- ❏ *Taraxacum officinale* common dandelion
- ❏ *Wyethia angustifolia* California compassplant

Berberidaceae

- ❏ ***Berberis nervosa*** Cascade barberry, p. 12

Betulaceae

- ❏ ***Alnus rubra*** red alder, p. 14
- ❏ *Corylus cornuta* ssp. *californica* California hazelnut

Blechnaceae

- ❑ ***Woodwardia fimbriata*** giant chainfern, p. 80

Boraginaceae

- ❑ ***Cynoglossum grande*** Pacific hound's tongue, p. 71
- ❑ *Eriodictyon californicum* California yerba santa
- ❑ ***Myosotis latifolia*** broadleaf forget-me-not, p. 72
- ❑ *Myosotis sylvatica* woodland forget-me-not

Brassicaceae

- ❑ *Brassica nigra* black mustard
- ❑ *Brassica rapa* field mustard
- ❑ ***Cardamine californica*** milkmaids, p. 37
- ❑ *Cardamine californica* var. *integrifolia* milkmaids
- ❑ *Erysimum capitatum* coast wallflower
- ❑ *Erysimum franciscanum* San Francisco wallflower
- ❑ *Raphanus sativus* garden radish
- ❑ *Thysanocarpus curvipes* lacepod mustard

Campanulaceae

- ❑ *Campanula prenanthoides* California harebell
- ❑ *Heterocodon rariflorum* western pearlflower

Caprifoliaceae

- ❑ ***Lonicera hispidula*** pink honeysuckle, p. 15
- ❑ *Lonicera involucrata* bearberry honeysuckle
- ❑ *Symphoricarpos albus* var. *laevigatus* common snowberry
- ❑ *Symphoricarpos mollis* creeping snowberry

Caryophyllaceae

- ❑ *Silene gallica* common catchfly
- ❑ *Spergularia rubra* purple sandspurry
- ❑ *Stellaria media* chickweed

Celastraceae

- ❑ ***Euonymus occidentalis*** western burning bush, p. 16

Convolvulaceae

- ❑ ***Calystegia occidentalis*** chaparral false bindweed, p. 38
- ❑ * *Calystegia purpurata* Pacific false bindweed
- ❑ * *Cuscuta californica* California dodder
- ❑ *Dichondra donnelliana* California dichondra

Cornaceae

- ❑ *Cornus sericea* redosier dogwood

Crassulaceae

- ❑ * *Dudleya farinosa* powdery liveforever

Cucurbitaceae

- ❑ *Marah fabaceus* California manroot

- ❑ ***Marah oregana*** coastal manroot, p. 39

Cupressaceae

- ❑ *Callitropsis macrocarpa* Monterey cypress
- ❑ ***Sequoia sempervirens*** coast redwood, p. 17

Cyperaceae

- ❑ *Carex globosa* roundfruit sedge
- ❑ * *Cyperus esculentus* yellow nutgrass

Dennstaedtiaceae

- ❑ ***Pteridium aquilinum* var. *pubescens*** western brackenfern, p. 82

Dryopteridaceae

- ❑ * ***Dryopteris arguta*** coastal woodfern, p. 83
- ❑ ***Polystichum dudleyi*** Dudley's sword fern, p. 84
- ❑ ***Polystichum munitum*** western swordfern, p. 84

Equisetaceae

- ❑ ***Equisetum telmateia* ssp. *braunii*** giant horsetail, p. 86

Ericaceae

- ❑ *Arbutus menziesii* Pacific madrone
- ❑ *Arctostaphylos glandulosa ssp. glandulosa* eastwood manzanita
- ❑ * *Arctostaphylos nummularia* glossyleaf manzanita
- ❑ *Arctostaphylos virgata* Marin manzanita
- ❑ * *Gaultheria shallon* salal
- ❑ *Rhododendron macrophyllum* California rhododendron
- ❑ ***Rhododendron occidentale*** California azalea, p. 19
- ❑ *Vaccinium ovatum* California huckleberry
- ❑ *Vaccinium parvifolium* red huckleberry

Fabaceae

- ❑ * *Acacia dealbata* mimosa
- ❑ *Acacia farnesiana* sweet acacia
- ❑ *Acacia melanoxylon* Australian blackwood
- ❑ *Cytisus scoparius* Scotch broom
- ❑ *Genista monspessulana* Cape broom
- ❑ *Lathyrus latifolius* giant pea
- ❑ *Lotus corniculatus* birdfoot trefoil
- ❑ * *Lotus micranthus* desert deervetch
- ❑ *Lupinus arboreus* yellow bush lupine
- ❑ *Lupinus bicolor* bicolor lupine
- ❑ * *Medicago polymorpha* bur clover
- ❑ *Pickeringia montana* chaparral pea
- ❑ *Spartium junceum* Spanish broom
- ❑ *Thermopsis macrophylla* false lupine
- ❑ *Vicia americana* American vetch
- ❑ *Vicia sativa* common vetch

Fagaceae

- ❑ *Chrysolepis chrysophylla* var. *chrysophylla* giant chinquapin
- ❑ *Chrysolepis chrysophylla* var. *minor* giant chinquapin
- ❑ ***Lithocarpus densiflorus*** tanoak, p. 20
- ❑ *Quercus agrifolia* var. *agrifolia* California live oak
- ❑ *Quercus chrysolepis* canyon live oak
- ❑ * *Quercus parvula* var. *shrevei* Shreve's oak
- ❑ * *Quercus wislizeni* var. *frutescens* interior live oak
- ❑ * *Quercus wislizeni* var. *wislizeni* interior live oak

Garryaceae

- ❑ *Garrya elliptica* wavyleaf silktassel

Geraniaceae

- ❑ *Erodium botrys* longbeak stork's bill
- ❑ *Erodium cicutarium* redstem filaree
- ❑ * *Geranium dissectum* cutleaf geranium
- ❑ *Geranium molle* awnless geranium
- ❑ *Geranium pusillum* small-flower crane's-bill

Grossulariaceae

- ❑ *Ribes menziesii* canyon gooseberry
- ❑ *Ribes sanguineum* redflower currant
- ❑ *Ribes sanguineum* var. *glutinosum* blood currant

Hydrangeaceae

- ❑ ***Whipplea modesta*** modesty (historical records only), p. 40

Hydrophyllaceae

- ❑ *Nemophila menziesii* baby blue eyes
- ❑ *Phacelia californica* California phacelia

Hypericaceae

- ❑ * *Hypericum perforatum* common St. John's wort

Iridaceae

- ❑ *Crocosmia* × *crocosmiiflora* crocosmia
- ❑ ***Iris douglasiana*** Douglas iris, p. 73
- ❑ *Iris macrosiphon* bowltube iris
- ❑ ***Sisyrinchium bellum*** western blue-eyed grass, p. 74

Juncaceae

- ❑ *Juncus patens* spreading rush

Lamiaceae

- ❑ ***Clinopodium douglasii*** yerba buena, p. 41
- ❑ ***Lepechinia calycina*** pitcher sage, p. 21
- ❑ *Marrubium vulgare* horehound
- ❑ *Mentha pulegium* pennyroyal
- ❑ *Mentha* × *piperita* peppermint

- ❏ *Stachys ajugoides* bugle hedgenettle
- ❏ *Stachys bullata* California hedgenettle
- ❏ ***Stachys rigida*** rough hedgenettle, p. 59

Lauraceae

- ❏ ***Umbellularia californica*** California laurel, p. 22

Liliaceae

- ❏ *Calochortus umbellatus* Oakland mariposa lily
- ❏ ***Clintonia andrewsiana*** Andrew's clintonia, p. 60
- ❏ ***Fritillaria affinis*** Mission bells, p. 76
- ❏ ***Lilium pardalinum*** leopard lily, p. 54
- ❏ *Prosartes hookeri* drops-of-gold
- ❏ ***Prosartes smithii*** large-flower fairybells, p. 42
- ❏ ***Scoliopus bigelovii*** California fetid adder's-tongue, p. 77

Linaceae

- ❏ *Linum bienne* pale flax

Malvaceae

- ❏ *Sidalcea malviflora* California checkerbloom

Melanthiaceae

- ❏ ***Toxicoscordion fremontii*** Fremont's deathcamas
- ❏ *Trillium chloropetalum* giant wakerobin
- ❏ ***Trillium ovatum*** Pacific trillium, p. 44
- ❏ *Xerophyllum tenax* common beargrass

ABOVE Giant Wakerobin (*Trillium chloropetalum*)

Montiaceae

- ❏ ***Claytonia perfoliata*** miner's lettuce, p. 45

Myrtaceae

- ❏ *Eucalyptus globulus* bluegum eucalyptus
- ❏ *Eucalyptus viminalis* manna gum

Onagraceae

- ❏ *Clarkia purpurea ssp. purpurea* winecup clarkia
- ❏ * *Clarkia purpurea ssp. viminea* winecup clarkia
- ❏ *Taraxia ovata* goldeneggs

Orchidaceae

- ❏ *Corallorrhiza maculata* spotted coralroot
- ❏ ***Corallorrhiza striata*** striped coralroot, p. 61
- ❏ *Goodyera oblongifolia* rattlesnake plantain
- ❏ *Piperia elegans* elegant piperia

Orobanchaceae

- ❏ ***Castilleja subinclusa* ssp. *franciscana*** longleaf Indian paintbrush, p. 62
- ❏ ***Pedicularis densiflora*** Indian-warrior, p. 63

Oxalidaceae

- ❏ ***Oxalis oregana*** redwood-sorrel, p. 64

- ❑ *Oxalis pes-caprae* African woodsorrel

Papaveraceae

- ❑ * *Dicentra formosa* Pacific bleeding heart
- ❑ ***Eschscholzia californica*** California poppy, p. 55
- ❑ *Platystemon californicus* California creamcups

Phrymaceae

- ❑ ***Mimulus aurantiacus*** sticky monkey flower, p. 56
- ❑ ***Mimulus cardinalis*** crimson monkeyflower, p. 65
- ❑ *Mimulus guttatus* common monkeyflower

Pinaceae

- ❑ *Pinus radiata* Monterey pine
- ❑ *Pseudotsuga menziesii* Douglas-fir

Plantaginaceae

- ❑ *Plantago erecta* dotseed plantain
- ❑ *Plantago lanceolata* lanceleaf plantain
- ❑ *Plantago major* common plantain

Poaceae

- ❑ *Aira caryophyllea* silver hairgrass
- ❑ *Briza maxima* big quakinggrass
- ❑ *Briza minor* little quakinggrass
- ❑ *Bromus carinatus* California brome
- ❑ *Bromus diandrus* ripgut brome
- ❑ *Bromus hordeaceus* soft chess
- ❑ *Cortaderia jubata* Andean pampas grass
- ❑ *Cynosurus echinatus* bristly dogstail grass
- ❑ *Danthonia californica* California oatgrass
- ❑ *Deschampsia elongata* slender hairgrass
- ❑ *Elymus californicus* California bottlebrush grass
- ❑ *Elymus elymoides* var. *californicus*
- ❑ *Elymus glaucus* ssp. *glaucus* blue wild rye
- ❑ * *Elymus glaucus* ssp. *virescens* blue wildrye
- ❑ *Elymus multisetus* big squirreltail
- ❑ *Festuca arundinacea* tall fescue
- ❑ *Festuca idahoensis* Idaho fescue
- ❑ *Gastridium ventricosum* nit grass
- ❑ *Hierochloe occidentalis* California sweetgrass
- ❑ *Holcus lanatus* common velvetgrass
- ❑ *Hordeum brachyantherum* meadow barley
- ❑ *Hordeum murinum* ssp. *leporinum* farmer's foxtail
- ❑ *Koeleria macrantha* junegrass
- ❑ *Melica californica* California melicgrass
- ❑ *Melica torreyana* Torrey's melicgrass

ABOVE Cone of Douglas-fir, a common evergreen tree in Muir Woods

- ❏ *Nassella pulchra* Purple needlegrass
- ❏ *Phalaris aquatica* bulbous canarygrass
- ❏ * *Poa pratensis* Kentucky bluegrass
- ❏ *Polypogon interruptus* ditch polypogon
- ❏ *Polypogon monspeliensis* rabbitfoot grass
- ❏ * *Vulpia myuros* foxtail fescue

Polemoniaceae

- ❏ *Navarretia squarrosa* skunkbush

Polygonaceae

- ❏ *Eriogonum latifolium* seaside buckwheat
- ❏ * *Rumex acetosella* sheep sorrel

Polypodiaceae

- ❏ ***Polypodium californicum*** California polypody, p. 87
- ❏ ***Polypodium glycyrrhiza*** licorice fern, p. 88
- ❏ ***Polypodium scouleri*** leathery polypody, p. 89

Primulaceae

- ❏ *Anagallis arvensis* pimpernel
- ❏ ***Dodecatheon hendersonii*** mosquito bills, p. 67
- ❏ ***Trientalis latifolia*** western starflower, p. 66

Pteridaceae

- ❏ ***Adiantum aleuticum*** Aleutian maidenhair, p. 90
- ❏ ***Adiantum jordanii*** California maidenhair fern, p. 91
- ❏ ***Pentagramma triangularis*** goldback fern, p. 92

Ranunculaceae

- ❏ ***Actaea rubra*** red baneberry, p. 46
- ❏ ***Anemone oregana*** blue windflower, p. 47
- ❏ *Aquilegia formosa* crimson columbine
- ❏ *Clematis ligusticifolia* virgin's-bower
- ❏ *Delphinium hesperium* foothill larkspur
- ❏ *Delphinium nudicaule* red larkspur
- ❏ ***Ranunculus californicus*** California buttercup, p. 57

Rhamnaceae

- ❏ ***Ceanothus thyrsiflorus*** blueblossom, p. 23
- ❏ *Frangula californica* ssp. *californica* California buckthorn

Rosaceae

- ❏ *Acaena pinnatifida* var. *californica* California sheepburr
- ❏ *Adenostoma fasciculatum* chamise
- ❏ * *Duchesnea indica* mock strawberry
- ❏ *Eriobotrya japonica* loquat
- ❏ ***Fragaria vesca*** woodland strawberry, p. 48
- ❏ ***Heteromeles arbutifolia*** toyon, 24

- ❏ *Holodiscus discolor* creambush
- ❏ *Horkelia californica* California horkelia
- ❏ *Rosa californica* California wildrose
- ❏ ***Rosa gymnocarpa*** dwarf rose, 25
- ❏ *Rubus discolor* Himalaya blackberry
- ❏ ***Rubus parviflorus*** western thimbleberry, p. 26
- ❏ *Rubus spectabilis* salmonberry
- ❏ ***Rubus ursinus*** California blackberry, p. 27

Rubiaceae

- ❏ *Galium aparine* bedstraw
- ❏ ***Galium triflorum*** fragrant bedstraw, p. 49

Salicaceae

- ❏ *Salix lasiolepis* arroyo willow

Sapindaceae

- ❏ *Acer macrophyllum* bigleaf maple
- ❏ ***Aesculus californica*** California buckeye, p. 28

ABOVE Bigleaf Maple (*Acer macrophyllum*)

Saxifragaceae

- ❏ *Boykinia occidentalis* coast boykinia
- ❏ ***Heuchera micrantha*** crevice alumroot, p. 50
- ❏ ***Lithophragma affine*** San Francisco woodland-star, p. 51
- ❏ ***Tellima grandiflora*** fringe cups, p. 68

Scrophulariaceae

- ❏ ***Scrophularia californica*** California figwort, p. 69

Solanaceae

- ❏ *Solanum americanum* American black nightshade

Taxaceae

- ❏ *Torreya californica* California nutmeg

Tropaeolaceae

- ❏ *Tropaeolum majus* nasturtium

Urticaceae

- ❏ ***Urtica dioica* ssp. *gracilis*** California nettle, p. 52

Violaceae

- ❏ ***Viola sempervirens*** evergreen violet, p. 58

Woodsiaceae

- ❏ ***Athyrium filix-femina* var. *cyclosorum*** subarctic ladyfern, p. 79
- ❏ * *Cystopteris fragilis* fragile fern

Notes

Index

www.ingramcontent.com/pod-product-compliance
Lightning Source LLC
Chambersburg PA
CBHW052118030426
42335CB00025B/3038
* 9 7 8 1 9 5 1 6 8 2 7 2 9 *